Mary Ann Beinecke

DIRECTOR, NANTUCKET SCHOOL OF NEEDLERY

BASIC NEEDLERY STITCHES
ON MESH FABRICS

Sponsored by
The Nantucket Historical Trust

DOVER PUBLICATIONS, INC.
NEW YORK

Dedicated to the teachers
who have tested and taught this course

Published in Canada by General Publishing Company, Ltd., 30
Lesmill Road, Don Mills, Toronto, Ontario.
Published in the United Kingdom by Constable and Company,
Ltd., 10 Orange Street, London WC 2.

Basic Needlery Stitches on Mesh Fabrics is a new work, first
published by Dover Publications, Inc., in 1973.

Acknowledgments. Design: Shaun Johnston. Production: Leonard
Roland. Photography: Bud Stockley.

International Standard Book Number: 0–486–21713–2
Library of Congress Catalog Card Number: 73–77444

Manufactured in the United States of America
Dover Publications, Inc.
180 Varick Street
New York, N.Y. 10014

What is the Nantucket School of Needlery?

The Nantucket School of Needlery is a non-profit, educational institution located on the island of Nantucket, Massachusetts. It is sponsored by The Nantucket Historical Trust. The teachers at the School are from Nantucket, trained by consultants from all over the world. Besides teaching the resident classes, workshops, and seminars, the Nantucket School of Needlery is licensed by the State of Massachusetts to teach through the mail with its Extension Course for Home Study, making it possible for an off-islander to qualify as a Needlery teacher. The School houses an important rare book library on textile and pure design. In order to encourage fine craftsmanship, good design, and discriminating use of color, the School researches and develops threads, yarns, fabrics, colorlines, dyes, stitches, and techniques. At the Nantucket School of Needlery, it is believed that all forms of needlework belong in a critical study of Needlery, and in the School's Extension Course for Home Study all are merely parts of the total flow of Needlery. At the School, itself, however, it has been possible to study Meshwork as a separate subject.

What is Meshwork and what are Mesh Stitches?

What is this book?

How is this book used?

MESH STITCHES ARE STANDARD NEEDLERY STITCHES, MADE COM-POUND BY COMBINATION WITH THEMSELVES OR OTHER STITCHES AND WORKED AS COUNTED STITCHES IN CLOSED FILLINGS. Stitches may be orderly or freely and unevenly worked. They may overlap. Meshwork is the skillful use of these stitches on a mesh whose lines of warp and weft threads and whose spaces are evenly distributed to the inch both horizontally and vertically and can be plainly seen.

THIS BOOK IS A WORKBOOK. IT IS A BEGINNING STUDY OF MESHWORK, the first of a series of lively books; it contains the Mesh Course #1 taught only at the Nantucket School of Needlery.

People who exclusively use the Tent Stitch and call it Needlepoint to execute pre-painted, pre-planned, pre-digested designs are not employing an adventurous approach to Meshwork. THIS BOOK IS for the person who is. It contains instructions for flat stitches, laced stitches, and the basic cross stitches. THIS BOOK IS for the person who wants to have fun while thinking and creating.

This book is used, not just read, not just studied. *Use it* effectively by initially following the teaching order from start to finish.

Use the graphs. It is important to graph stitches and patterns correctly. Any stitch reaches from the center of a space to the center of another space, a counted distance away, in a prescribed direction. Two adjoining stitches meet in the same space. If you draw the stitches on the graph paper as if the lines were the threads of the mesh and the spaces were the holes of the mesh, you will be able to accurately transfer this in yarn and threads to mesh. Do not color a space to represent a stitch. The left side of each left page has a graph printed on it. Graph the working of each stitch. On the first page, the graphing has been completed as an illustration.

Use the directions. Following horizontally across the page from the graph are, first, the explanation of the stitch, and, second, the illustration of the stitch keyed to the explanation. The illustration is worked both with a fine thread to define the exact relationship of each stitch to the others as well as to the mesh and, then, with a covering yarn to show the resultant texture. An "**A**" following a number indicates the needle coming up from the back to the surface and a "**B**" indicates the needle passing to the back. An "**a**" or a "**b**" indicates a second journey.

Record observations and comments. The character of a pattern must be analyzed. Observations such as whether a particular stitch or pattern can be worked on a diagonal or circular or straight design are necessary to record. Observations as to how two stitches join without awkwardly exposing the background fabric are necessary.

Use the sampler pattern. On the back of this book is a numbered, reduced pattern guide for a finished sampler. Each stitch or pattern in this book has a number which corresponds to an area on the pattern. As you finish studying

What about materials?

How should designs be applied to mesh?

a particular stitch, work it immediately on a sampler in the correct position. You will easily learn to apply guidelines to the mesh and adjust them according to the count mesh you use, to the size of the stitches you choose, and the size fabric you work.

The choice of yarns and threads and mesh is important for the various stitches to be seen as unique.

One size of yarn for one kind of stitch on one count mesh has been customarily used. As soon as a variety of stitches on differing counts of mesh are used, however, it becomes necessary to use a basic yarn that can be plyed up or down. A good worsted yarn should bite into the surface of the background fabric, never mat the texture of the stitches or "fluff up" on the surface. Rug mesh requires rug yarn. Metallics, silks, cottons, and linens all may be used. Exciting design requires an excited worker, eager to experiment with his materials. There are many qualities of mesh available. Never work on poor quality mesh. Mesh is designated by number: #6 is a large scale rug mesh, #10 a standard rug or wall hanging mesh, #12 an average, popular mesh, #18, fine. The best commercial mesh is woven of tightly twisted long staple linen, with little or no added sizing. Long staple cotton can also be a good mesh, as well as a combination of long staple cotton and linen. Mesh woven of a medium twisted long staple linen, available in colors, is excellent for restoration work or for pieces where some of the background fabric will show. A curtain might have only a border of Meshwork. Write to The Nantucket School of Needlery for further information about materials or answers to questions.

It is not desirable to paint designs on mesh. If you ever do want to color the mesh, do so lightly with acrylics. Any sort of paint shows through the stitches. As work progresses, changes may occur in color placement or stitch proportion. Often the stitch plan is not totally conceived beforehand and it is better to remain flexible. Draw designs on paper and paint them on the paper cartoons which should be, if possible, on graph paper whose count matches the mesh and whose all-over size is one to one, equal to the finished piece. There are three methods. One, is to use an indelible ink which will not wash out but may later be visible under a light colored yarn. Two, is to use a washable ink which may adhere to the yarn in the final washing, especially when coming from beneath a dense filling. The School advises a third, sewing thread, to divide the surface into graphed areas and to define shapes. As soon as one area is worked, the thread is removed. Look at the sampler pattern on the back of this book. To delineate this on any size background, stitch first one horizontal and one vertical guideline crossing at the center. Then, subdivide each quarter on exact straight lines. Following these, work the individual areas according to the measure of the stitch or pattern so the finished piece will be the result of the count of the stitches, themselves. Paper cartoons can be graphed and color coded stitch by stitch over the

What are good working habits?

horizontal and vertical intersections. From the cartoons, place guidelines and outlines on the mesh. By placing the mesh directly on top of the cartoon, the design is clearly seen through the spaces in the mesh. This can be accentuated by placing both over a light box. A light box is a box with lights inside illuminating a translucent glass top.

The first working habit is to not work on the mesh until the design has been conceived, in the proportions fitting to its end use, and color planned. Spend time on planning. Use colored papers of all kinds to test various combinations, and, finally, pastels, colored pencils, or paint on graph paper. Mistakes are avoided by using the same size graph paper as mesh count, eliminating conversions.

Always test stitches and threads and yarns first on a "doodle cloth." Decide on color combinations and textures, proportions, and plys before work on the final piece.

If possible, work in a frame. When linen thread is stretched, it does not go back into place. The mesh should be kept square at all times and never turned. Keep one hand below the frame and one above. Pass down from the surface and push up from the back in contrast to the whipping motion used when working "in the hand." The stitches will be sharply defined and evenly tensioned. Occasionally, let the needle dangle on the end of the yarn to untwist. Never allow the yarn to bunch. It should always be at ease. Use a smaller ply rather than one too heavy.

Never tie a knot in the yarn before starting. Secure the end by running the needle under existing stitches, or by taking a stitch around a thread at the back and then slipping the point of the needle through the body of the yarn (not the tail). When a yarn is finished, repeat either of these methods. Occasionally a stitch finishes in the same space the next one must begin. This is usually at the finish of one row and the start of the next. Simply loop the working thread around a thread of the mesh at the back after ending one row and then bring the needle right back up in the same space.

Choose needles carefully. A short, blunt needle with a large eye is required. The size must suit the thread or yarn. Finished pieces should be blocked and, preferably, washed. For blocking, dampen the back of the piece with a wet sponge. For washing, dip into and move gently about in a mild solution of Ivory Snow and rinse using tepid water. Squeeze, do not wring. In either case, have prepared a large wooden board, covered tautly with muslin. With rustproof tacks, tack the piece face up on the board, beginning with the corners diagonal to each other, followed by the center of the sides opposite one another. Build up until the entire piece is thoroughly secured on the square. After it has dried in place, pry up the tacks and the piece is ready for use.

BASIC NEEDLERY STITCHES
ON MESH FABRICS

Contents

Contents

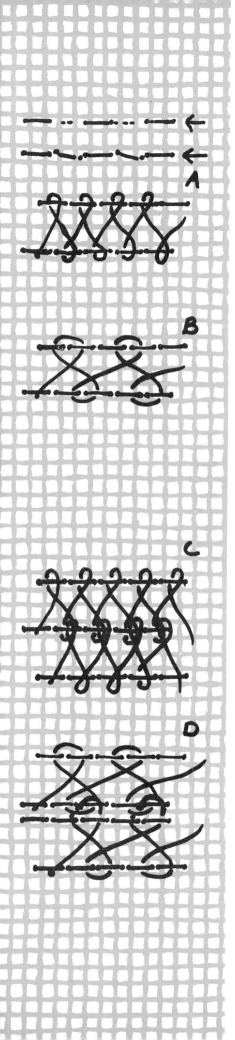

1. **The INTERLACED BAND starts with a row of Running Stitches, over an even number of threads, which defines the design line to be covered.** The Running Stitch is the most simple of the Needlery stitches. It travels always forward with the needle going over as many lines as it goes under. The Running Stitch becomes a Double Running Stitch when a second journey is carried back over the same row. In this journey the stitch lies on the surface where there was no thread from the Running Stitch and lies beneath the surface where there was a thread. When working these stitches, be careful to bring the needle out in the same space but just above the former stitch, **1A** and insert it, **1B**, in the same space but just below the next stitch, to maintain the appearance of an even row.

Work a second row of Double Running Stitches a measured distance below the first and in a bricked position in relation to the first row. This means that the space where two stitches meet is opposite the center of a stitch in the neighboring row.

We illustrate two basic methods of interlacing these two rows, **A** and **B**. Begin by bringing the interlacing thread up from beneath the center of the stitch furthest left on the left hand side of the two rows of stitches. In **A**, the interlacing thread is taken from one side forward over the top of the next stitch in the other row, back under this Running Stitch, over the previous working thread and back to the beginning row. In **B**, the working thread is taken from one side forward to the following stitch in the opposing row where it goes under this thread and back under the previous Running Stitch before being taken over the working thread and back to the beginning row.

In actually working this Band you will no doubt find that the yarn used for the interlacing must be plyed up to adequately cover the background mesh. Note carefully the differences between these methods.

When the Interlaced Band is used for a solid filling, it is necessary to attach the bands. The first band, **C**, is repeated by working a third row of Double Running Stitch identical to the first and bricked to the second. As this second band is interlaced, the needle goes through the loop of the previous interlacing as well as over and under the Running Stitches. The second band, **D**, requires a third row of Double Running Stitches immediately below the second, not bricked, and then a fourth, bricked, measured down the same distance as between the first and the second. After the working thread is interlaced under the first stitch in the opposing row and before it passes back under the previous Running Stitch in that same row, it catches, by going down through, the base of the interlacing loop from the previous row.

You can see that not only does the interlacing, itself, appear different in **D** than in **C**, but a striped effect occurs as well as a wavy line between the two close rows of Double Running Stitches. At the School, **C** is named "Angie's Way" and **D**, "Petty's Way." There are some other variations which you may be able to invent once you have closely observed and understood the workings of these principles.

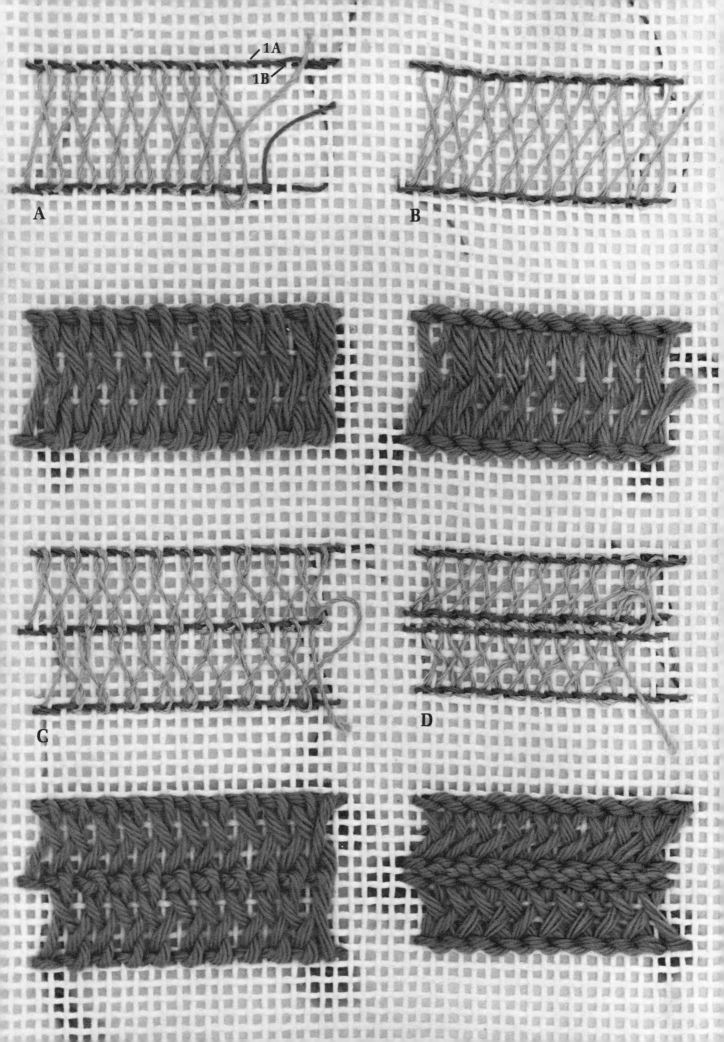

GOBELIN PATTERNS are solid fillings of bricked stitches.

2. **GOBELIN PATTERN, VERTICAL is worked using differing methods.** There is an arrow pointing to the beginning of each first stitch in the illustration of each method. Upright stitches may be worked in rows of Double Running Stitch, each row bricked, **A**. Gobelin Pattern, Vertical may be worked in horizontal, enmeshed rows of vertical stitches. Each stitch can be worked from the top to the bottom, **B**, or, to economize thread, one stitch may be worked from the top to the bottom and the next from the bottom to the top in a threading rhythm, **C**. The rhythm of **B**, a whipping motion, is the better with which to maintain even tension. Shading of one horizontal row after another is better worked with either **B** or **C** method. Shading of one vertical row after another is better worked with **A** method. It is also possible, of course, to work diagonal rows, **D**.

3. **GOBELIN PATTERN, HORIZONTAL is worked with any of the methods of the Gobelin Filling, Vertical, also over an even line count, E.** When working in rows, remember to leave a space between stitches for the neighboring enmeshed rows. Gobelin Filling, Horizontal seems to need a heavier plyed yarn to cover the mesh completely than does the Gobelin Pattern, Vertical.

4. **GOBELIN PATTERN, DIAGONAL, is worked over an uneven number of intersections; these intersections lie on a straight diagonal, F.** It is important to work this filling one diagonal row of diagonal stitches at a time over the uneven count of intersections. It is also important to hold the mesh in an upright position. Each stitch in each row is placed diagonally next to the preceding stitch. Note in the illustration that this does leave space for the subsequent enmeshed row.

When the various Gobelin Patterns abut one another, adjoining rows encroach to prevent mesh showing through the covering yarn. This means that the start of any of the abutting stitches actually emerges from the back *under* a stitch from the first area covered by another type of Gobelin Pattern.

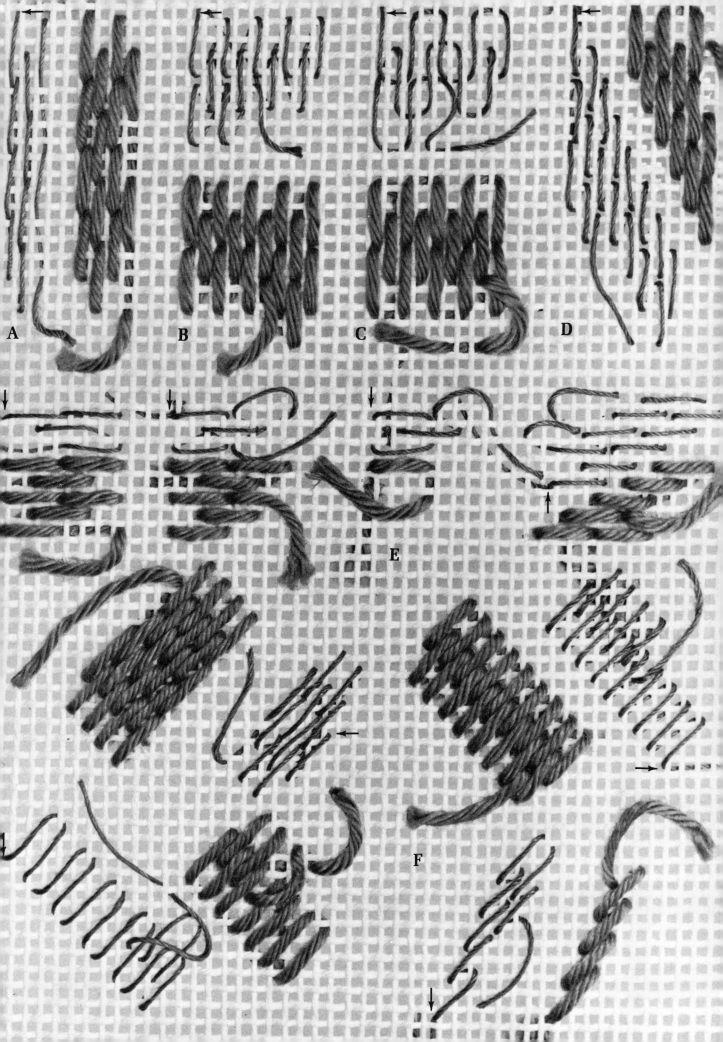

A

B

C

D

E

F

5. The DOUBLE FLAT STITCH is essentially a band stitch, an Open Gobelin Filling; many variations may be devised.

One is composed of band upon band. The Double Flat Stitch is a Darning Stitch that turns back upon itself. Consequently, it moves always forward in a threading motion, not a whipping motion, **A**. Begin at the base of the twin stitches, **1A**, take one upright stitch over an even number of lines, **1B**, pass beneath an even number of lines and work another twin stitch above the first, **2A-2B**. Reverse direction, work one stitch, **3A-3B**, that begins and ends next to the center of the two previous stitches, and begin the cycle once more. The open areas may be filled with yarns of other colors whose length depends on the count of the uncovered lines. Half of the illustration is filled.

Combine staggered rows of Double Flat Stitch, **B**, enabling the twin stitches from one row to move into the openings between the central stitches of neighboring rows. The only empty areas in this variation are those between the pairs of twin stitches. These are of one length, in staggered horizontal rows. Thread or lace ribbons, sticks, or yarns under the single stitches or fill the openings with additional stitches.

The preceding two variations may be worked on the diagonal, **C**. The ends of the twin stitches are worked into successive diagonal spaces instead of alternate spaces. Each stitch is over an uneven count of lines.

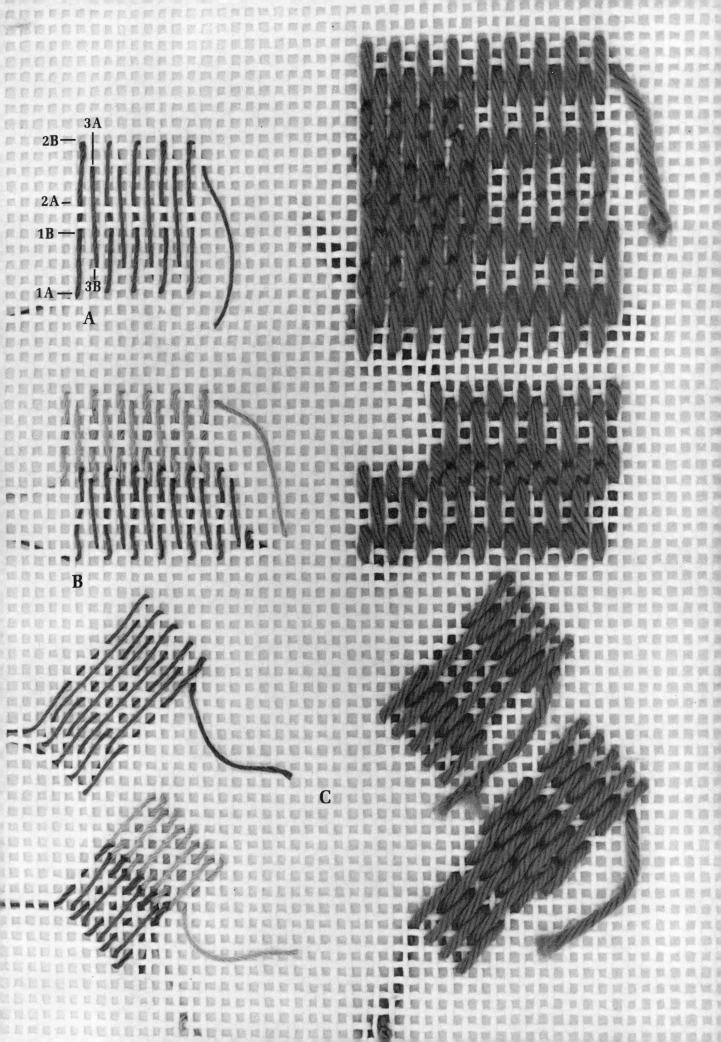

6. **The STEM STITCH and the WIDE STEM STITCH are the same.** The Stem Stitch is worked into one row of spaces and the Wide Stem Stitch between adjacent rows of spaces. **A** illustrates the working of a Stem Stitch in one row. The rhythm is one of reaching all the way forward and coming halfway back. **1A-1B** is not pulled up until after the needle emerges at **2A**. The working thread is kept to one side, consistently, either above or below the row. When the Stem Stitch is worked between adjacent rows, it becomes the Wide Stem Stitch, **B**. The final appearance is that of a rope. Reversing direction every row results in another effect, **C**.

7. **The KNITTING PATTERN is simple to work and is texturally effective.** The result does resemble plain knitting. As is clearly illustrated, **D**, the entire Knitting Pattern is composed of two opposing rows of Wide Stem Stitches that share the central row of spaces. The previous stitch, therefore, is always held to the outside of the pair of rows as the work progresses. The flow of the stitches in the pairs is in one direction, but it is an easy matter to work from either direction by reversing the order. This is a good shading stitch.

8. **The ALTERNATING STEM STITCH is a simple Stem Stitch in which each alternate stitch is taken while the working thread is held up and the others while the thread is held down, E.** Like all Stem Stitches, the row progresses from the left to the right. Despite being worked in one row of mesh, the finished effect is of two rows of stitches. It is better as a filling if each successive row is worked the reverse of the preceding one, providing a surface of bricked pairs of stitches.

9. **The LOOPED ALTERNATING STEM STITCH is a fascinating stitch with many possibilities.** It is basically the same as the Alternating Stem Stitch. Each time the working thread is held either up (or down) it is held as a loop while the next stitch is taken *around* the right side of the loop and the following line of mesh. The row must begin with a securing stitch because this holds the left side of the loop. The illustration **F** shows first, the structure of the row with retaining stitches and loops; then, the row after each loop is cut in the center. After the loops are cut, note that the result is a looped knot over the mesh securing two yarn ends. This is the carpet knot known as the Smyrna Knot. It has many uses for effective Needlery because it can be left as a looped surface, **G**, or cut as a velvet surface, **H**, or pulled flat as the Alternating Stem Stitch, **I**. These variations may occur wherever needed to create patterns. Work loop or cut loop rows in consecutive rows of mesh or, for less density, separated by rows of the Alternating Stem Stitch as in **A** and **H**. Staggering the start of each row evenly on a diagonal creates a different surface than that resulting from rows which start each above the other, **J**. Loops worked in successive rows from the top of an area to the bottom have a particular slant which differs from that of loops worked from the bottom of an area to the top. This creates the "nap" with which everyone is familiar in a pile surface. The final looped pile surface may be sculptured into patterns with a sharply pointed scissor, **K**. This and the Alternating Stem Stitch are useful surfaces because of the possible textural variations as well as shape and color variations. Differing stitch lengths may be combined for added interest or pattern.

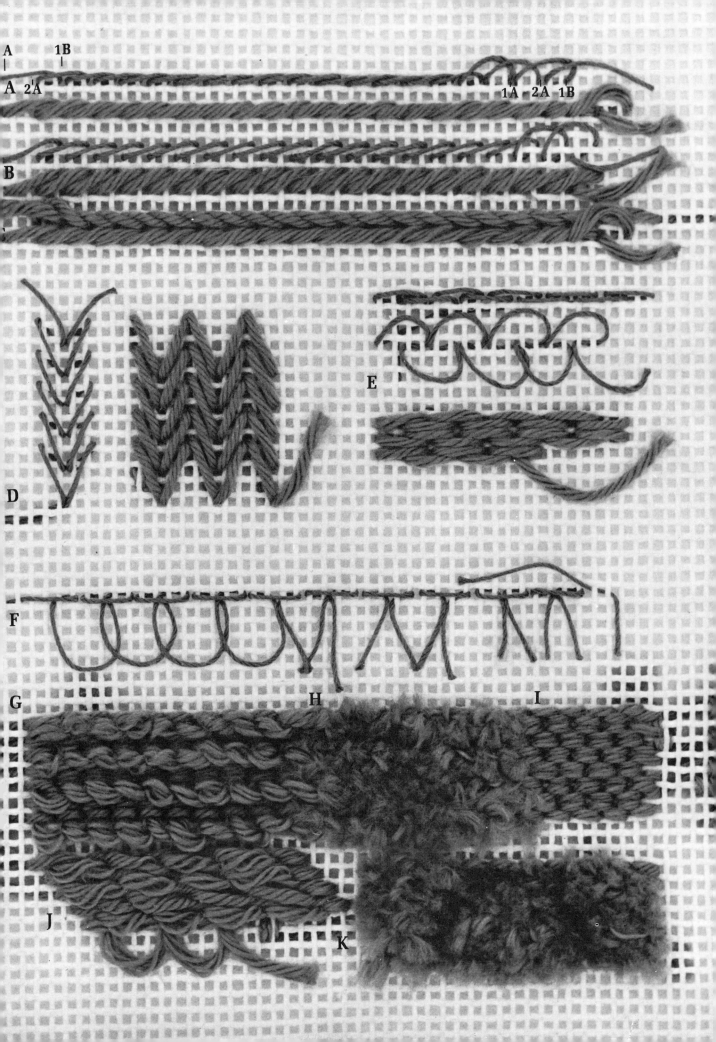

10. **The DOUBLE OPEN STEM STITCH is a Stem Stitch in which its rhythm and working order remain the same, but its individual stitches alternate between two rows.** The needle emerges in an adjoining row rather than beneath the former stitch. The entire repeat of two worked rows cover three neighboring rows of spaces in the mesh. Each second row begins two spaces apart from the first and they both share the center row. Consequently, the center row holds a double stitch; this creates a high and low surface texture that is pleasing. The yarn usually has to be plyed up for successful coverage. Working of the two journeys for one entire repeat is illustrated, **A**, in fine thread and two complete repeats in covering thread.

11. **The WOVEN STEM STITCH is a fascinating stitch which creates a strong, hardwearing, interwoven surface.** Startling texture and color effects are possible using this stitch. It is basically an Open Alternating Stem Stitch worked in four journeys. There is the possibility of using one to four different colors in any combination. We used two in alternation. The stitch is worked between two separated rows so the height of the row as well as the size of each stitch are for you to determine. Since there are four journeys, the space between stitches in the first journey must be equal to three stitches. Yarn must be plyed down for this stitch so as not to appear bunchy. The start and the finish of each row have beginning and finishing "tails" of stitches so in designing, plan to initially work the Woven Stem Stitch so these "tails" will be covered by the stitches of contiguous areas. The appearance of the filling depends on whether successive rows are begun even, vertically, or not.

Illustrations **B**, **C**, **D**, **E** show each successive journey. Note that the current working yarn in the needle is *always passed beneath the last thread from a previous journey.* It crosses all but the last previous thread. Note, also, that the thread leading from the preceding stitch is held to the outside of the row.

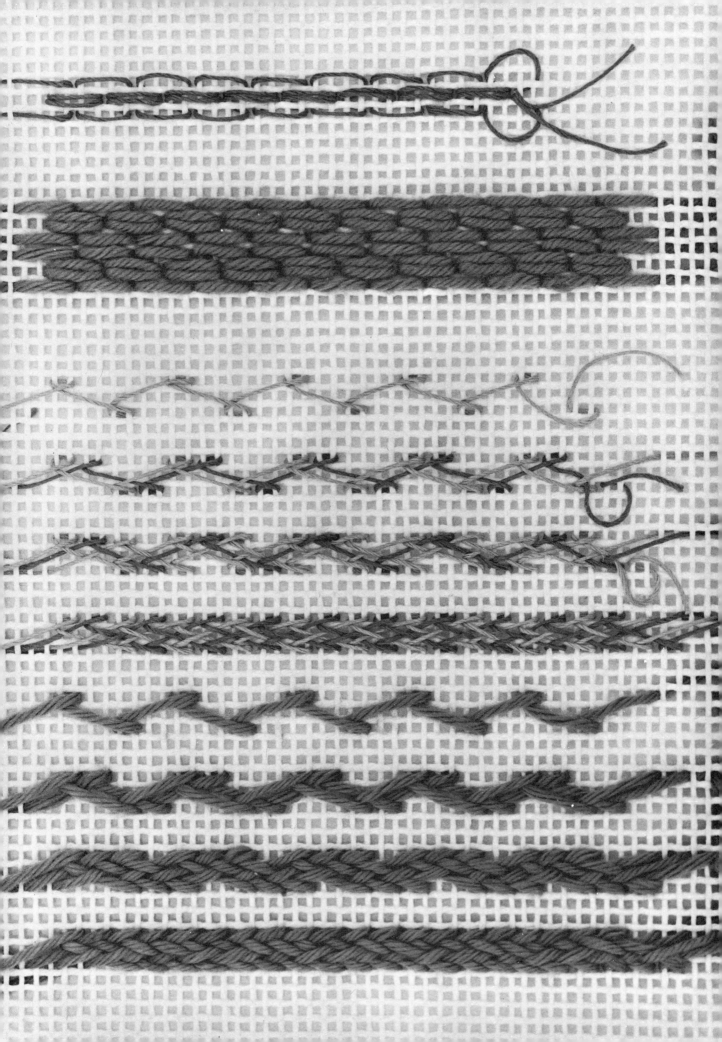

12. **The HUNGARIAN PATTERN, is composed of three stitches—one long and, on either side, two, one-half its length.** The three finish by appearing like a Cross Stitch, horizontal, vertical, or diagonal. First, **A**, work the middle long stitch, then the small stitch on the beginning side of the diagonal row, and last, the small stitch on the opposite side of the long stitch. Each stitch should be worked from the outside to the inside in the direction of the diagonal row; e.g., **1A-1B, 2A-2B, 3A-3B.** Be careful not to pull the mesh tightly. The crossed stitches on the back of the mesh help to distinctly unite the three stitches. Long stitches lie next to each other, short stitches lie next to each other. It is good technique to bring the needle out below the yarn of a preceding stitch and back above the next so that the stitches are clean and the yarns unsplit. Entire patterns and pictures may be stitched with the Hungarian Pattern, changing color wherever necessary, even in the middle of a unit. The central long stitch of a new unit is begun in a space next to the middle of the last stitch of the just completed unit.

HUNGARIAN PATTERN, HORIZONTAL, is worked as illustrated, B, in diagonal rows. For horizontal rows of self-color, **C**, work one unit, find the space where the next unit would have begun, count over two intersections on the diagonal to locate the following isolated unit in the correct spaces. Later, fill in with another color.

13. **HUNGARIAN PATTERN, VERTICAL, D, is worked using all the identical rules that apply to the Horizontal Hungarian.** The diagonal rows travel either to the left or to the right.

14. **HUNGARIAN PATTERN, DIAGONAL, utilizes stitches on the diagonal, E.** It is logical, therefore, that the count as well as the rows will travel on the verticals and the horizontals. The count of stitch lengths will be less on the diagonal to finish nearly the same size as the Horizontal or Vertical. The former may have been over 4 and 2 and on the Diagonal might be over 2 and 1 intersections. How do you finish the last unit in a row to establish a smooth diagonal join? Four units may join in a double inversion, so the long stitches of each unit radiate out from a common center, **F**. Another interesting effect is obtained by working one unit of diagonal stitches to the right and the next vertical unit of diagonal stitches to the left, **G**.

15. **The PRINCESS PATTERN is made of graduated, whipped vertical stitches from a horizontal base.** It may be varied in any proportion or size. First, work a horizontal row of stitches, each of which begins from a common base, **A**. The stitches are taken over one weft, over two, over three, over two, over one, over two, etc. After this row is finished, a mirror image is worked down from the base. Neighboring units share the first and last stitch. The Princess Pattern is completed by working a series of Back Stitches in fine yarn across the base. A Back Stitch is the reverse side of a Stem Stitch. It begins one stitch length in from the right side, **1A**, ends, **1B**, and begins the next stitch one more stitch length along the row, to the left. The use of varied colors changes the appearance. If more than one color is used in a horizontal row, a decision must be made about which unit includes the shared stitch.

16. **The UPRIGHT GOBELIN, of all mesh stitches, most accurately resembles tapestry weaving.** It is a straight, vertical stitch over, usually, two weft threads. It can be worked from left to right and, then, right to left, **B**, with each stitch taken from the bottom **1A**, to the top, **1B**. In this way subsequent rows remain neat because the needle goes down through the base of the stitch above and does not push up any threads from that stitch. It is possible to work this stitch on the diagonal, **C**. After finishing one stitch from bottom to top, **1A-1B**, cross under two warp threads to locate the next stitch **2A-2B**. The stitches on the down journey lie immediately to the left of the stitches in the rows previously established. To economize yarn, these stitches will be worked from the top, **3A-3B**, leaving horizontal and separated rows on the back. In this manner all the stitches that go into worked spaces travel from the front to the back. The rows may slant up to the left or right; subsequent down rows may be placed on either side of a previous row; all the same rules apply. As with any upright stitch, care must be exercised not to pull the stitch tight, thereby exposing the background mesh.

17. **The PADDED UPRIGHT GOBELIN STITCH is substituted for the Upright Gobelin Stitch, which has a tendency to appear messy unless a heavy yarn is used.** The final appearance is enhanced by padding the areas before stitching and we definitely recommend the technique. Cover each row between weft threads with loose, self-colored yarns laid horizontally. Stagger the starts and finishes of these padding yarns by using a Stem Stitch anchored irregularly over one or two intersections, **D**. Besides providing uniform coverage, this method emphasizes the ridged, grosgrain effect.

An interesting treatment of a design surface can be obtained using this method like the true tapestry technique. Wherever the pattern calls for it, change the color of the individual Upright Gobelin Stitches.

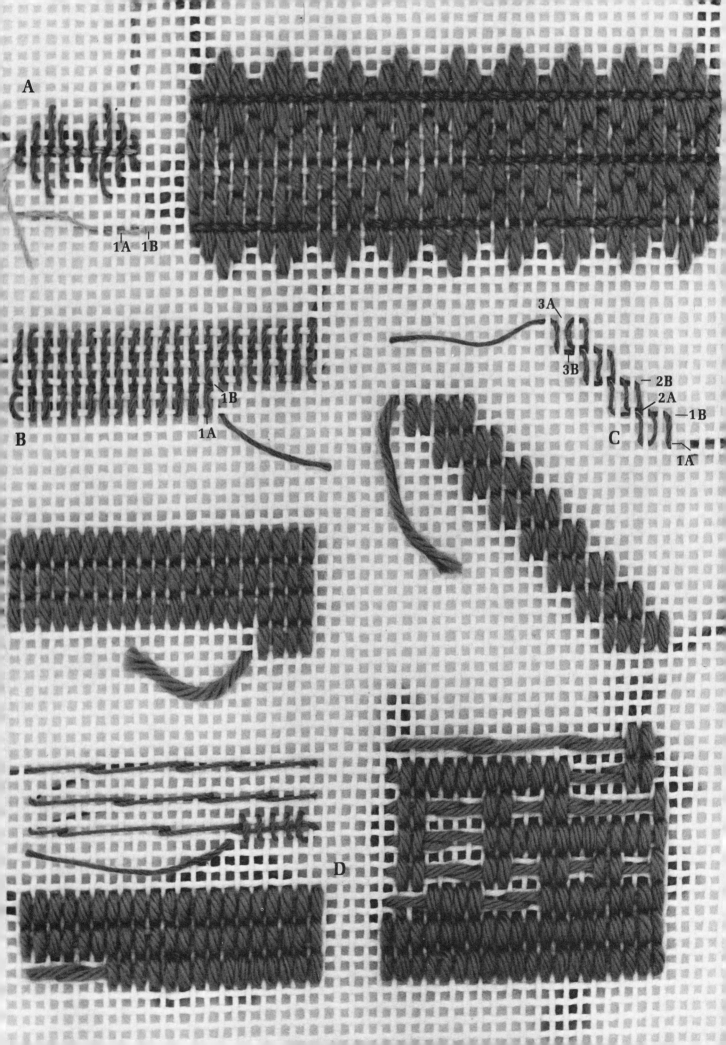

18. **The PARISIAN PATTERN is formed from horizontal as well as vertical rows of alternating long and short stitches.** The short stitch must be able to center on the long one, as when combining a stitch over two threads with one over four threads. The stitches may be worked along horizontal or vertical rows, **A**. Always plan subsequent rows to place the "**B**" half of the stitch into a space already occupied by a stitch. If an initial row has been worked from left to right with stitches worked from the bottom to the top, the next row is placed either above or below. If above, that row traveling from the right to the left should be composed of stitches worked from top to bottom.

It is simple to work the Parisian Pattern on the diagonal. As always, a long stitch alternates with a short. Begin with a long stitch, **1A-1B**, pass the needle horizontally under two warp threads on a level with **1B** and work the short stitch, **2A-2B**. When the border of the area has been reached, proceed with the down journey by working the stitches in reverse order, **3A-3B**. Begin the down journey with a stitch on one side of the last one of the preceding row. If on the inside, **B**, the row builds above the previous one; if on the outside, **C**, it builds below. In the illustrations with covering thread, **1A** is marked with an arrow. If the down journey begins with a stitch above or below the last one, every other vertical row remains empty, **D**. These might be filled with another type of stitch or a continuation of the Parisian Pattern in another color, or, perhaps, be threaded with novelty yarns, ribbons, straws, or grasses.

A

D C B

3A
3B
2B
1B
2A
1A

The **TENT STITCH** is sometimes referred to as Petit Point or Needlepoint. It is a single diagonal stitch usually slanted from lower left to upper right over the intersection of a warp and a weft thread, **A**. The relative size of a stitch is governed by the count of the mesh. The slant may be reversed to fit the pattern but whichever is chosen must be the slant of all the stitches in one area. The Tent Stitch is actually the last half of a Cross Stitch; since it was traditional for the last stitch of a Cross Stitch to cross from lower left to upper right, it became traditional for the Tent Stitch to do the same. The Cross Stitch is Gros Point; the Tent Stitch is Petit Point.

The Tent Stitch has no real character of its own. Consequently, choose it for flat, stylized designs as well as representational, "picture" designs. The highs and lows of a color are accentuated by the repeated bumps on the surface, reflecting light from the highest and shade from the lowest part of the stitch as the yarn goes to the back of the mesh. It is important to use a yarn that retains the individual shape of each stitch, having many "highs" and "lows" of its own.

There are several ways to work the Tent Stitch; they are all variations of the Back Stitch which pulls securely against itself. The method used should suit the circumstance. There is no one correct method. Note that this stitch is not a perfect choice for patterns because it is an unbalanced, directional stitch rather than one based on the square of the mesh. A diagonal to the right forms a straight line while a diagonal to the left forms a saw-toothed edge. One line, only, of stitches to the left do not join or touch. In designing on graph paper for the Tent Stitch, be certain to use a slanted line over an intersection, from the center of one space to the center of the next, to show the true relationships of the stitches.

19. **The CONTINENTAL TENT STITCH pulls against itself for desired even tension.** The row begins at the right with the first stitch, **1A-1B**. The needle passes behind this stitch as well as two warp threads to emerge in the space to the left of **1A** for **2A**, the beginning of the following stitch. End the row at the left side and begin once more on the right, **B**, or work from the left side back to the right side with Tent Stitches in reverse. Begin each stitch in the upper right and end in the lower left, **C**. The Continental Tent Stitch may also be worked vertically from the bottom to the top, **D**, or from the top to the bottom, **E**. Combining the two continuously fills an area with covering thread, as illustrated.

20. **The DIAGONAL TENT STITCH is worked with Back Stitches placed along a true diagonal of the mesh.** If all the individual stitches are to slant from lower left to upper right, these diagonal rows of Back Stitches may travel from the upper right of an area to the lower left, **F**, or from the lower left to the upper right, in reverse, **G**. In **H**, the two in combination have been used.

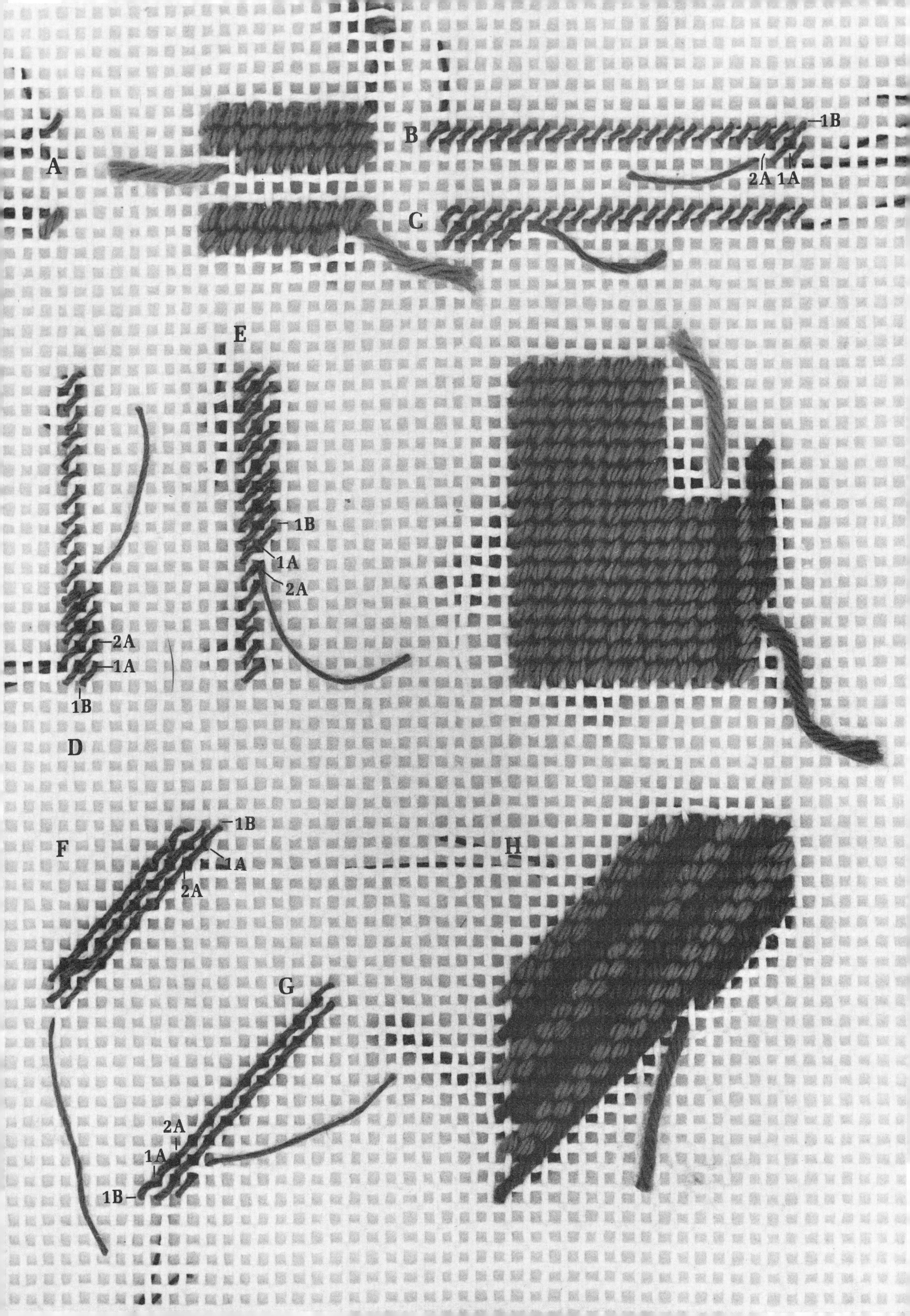

A

B

C —1B

2A 1A

E

—1B

1A

2A

2A

1A

1B

D

F —1B

1A

2A

H

G

2A

1A

1B—

21. **The BASKETWEAVE TENT STITCH is chosen if the area is to be worked from the lower right to the upper left, or the reverse.** The Back Stitch cannot be utilized because the slant of the stitch, itself, is in the opposite direction of the row. A slight variation forms this new method which, instead of building up rows of Stem Stitch on the reverse, builds up what appears as an evenwoven surface, reinforcing and stabilizing the total fabric. This method of working the Tent Stitch develops quickly on flat patterned areas or background of one color. The Basketweave Tent Stitch may begin in any of the four corners but it is wise to initially learn to travel between the lower right and the upper left. Start with a Tent Stitch, **1A-1B A**. The same procedure of passing the needle behind the stitch and two warp threads is followed for the next stitch as for the Continental Tent Stitch. The difference is that, because the row is traveling diagonally between the lower right and the upper left, each subsequent stitch must be started one row up from the last with the working thread passing behind the space above the former stitch, or up over one weft thread, for **2A-2B**. The stitches of the initial row are separated. Work the first stitch of the down journey either to the left or directly below the final stitch of the first row if you are filling the area to the left, **B** and above or to the right of the final stitch, **C**, if you are filling the area to the right. If you simply reverse the working direction of the stitch as you did in the Continental, the back of the fabric will show duplicate horizontal stitches separated by one row. To build up the basketwoven back, work the stitch from the base to the top, **1a-1b**, and then pass the needle behind the stitch from the former row as well as two weft threads to emerge for the next stitch, **2a**. Next, learn to begin in the upper left corner for a down journey. Third, begin in the upper right corner and work to the lower left, **D**. The first stitch, **1A-1B**, fits into the corner. The second stitch immediately below starts the Basketweave Tent rhythm. Fourth, begin in the lower left corner to work to the upper right. The first stitch is in the corner, **1A-1B**, **E**. The second stitch to its right begins the Basketweave Tent. Finish by experimenting to fill an irregular area.

22. **The interesting and useful basketweave texture is built up on the surface in the REVERSE BASKETWEAVE TENT STITCH.** This is accomplished by working the Basketweave Tent Stitch from the underside of the mesh or, in a sense, upside down from the front. Our illustration has been worked with the mesh face up while the mind follows the rhythm of the Basketweave Tent Stitch on the back, **F**. On the up journey, exercise care to emerge to the left of the stitch from the previous row; on the down journey, emerge above the stitch from the previous row.

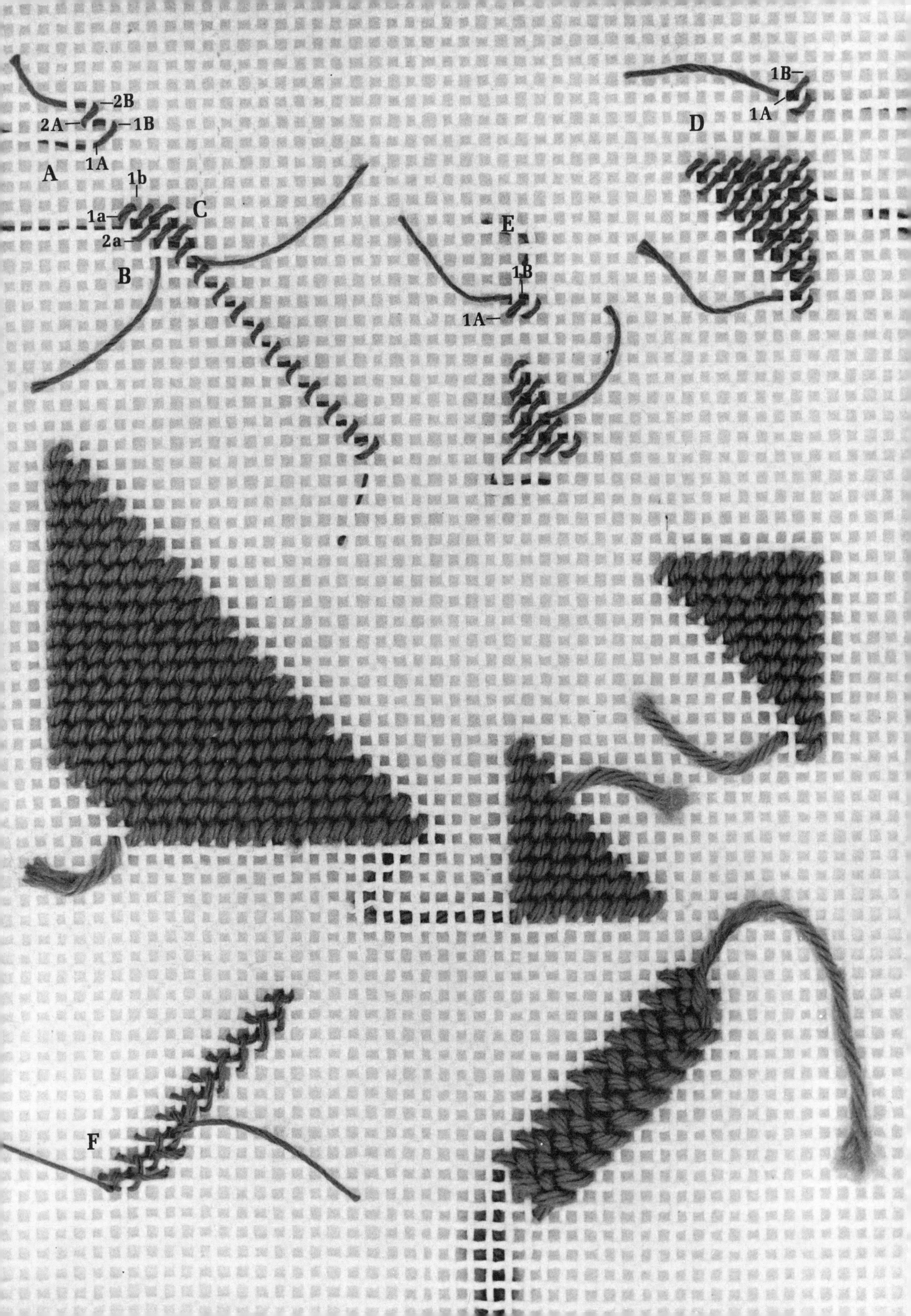

2B
2A
1B
1A
A
1b
1a
C
2a
B
1B
1A
D
E
1B
1A
F

23. **The CASHMERE PATTERN is composed of one Tent Stitch and two double Tent Stitches, or, of three diagonal stitches slanted from lower left to upper right; one, over one intersection and two, over two intersections, A.** The Cashmere Pattern is confusing only because of the order in which it is worked and the manner one row joins another. Look carefully at the illustration **B**. Do you see rectangles composed of two single stitches and two double stitches rather than units of three stitches? The single stitch seems always to be shared by neighboring pairs of double stitches. If you work from the top down, **1A-1B, 2A-2B, 3A-3B,** note that the three stitches are flush on the left. If you work from the bottom up, **1a-1b, 2a-2b, 3a-3b,** note that the three stitches are flush on the right. Rows are joined by placing the flush right unit to the left of a flush left unit, or vice versa. On the down journey the single stitch is a different one in relation to the two double stitches than on the up journey.

Since the Cashmere Pattern is composed of stitches on the true diagonal, it is possible to work this pattern diagonally with a Back Stitch, from upper right to lower left. The stitch count is in the same cycle, that of one single Tent Stitch followed by two double Tent Stitches, **C**. The first row is begun one space away from the upper right corner and worked in the order of one single Back Stitch, **1A-1B,** and two double Back Stitches, **2A-2B, 3A-3B.** The second row begins with the second stitch of the unit directly beneath the first of the initial row and is worked in the order of **2A-2B, 3A-3B, 1A-1B.** The third row completes the unit. It begins directly below the first stitch of the second row and is worked in the order of **3A-3B, 1A-1B, 2A-2B.** The fourth row begins the second unit so the starting position must be moved. This can be seen in the working diagram. In actual practice, the rows can be worked back and forth. Exercise care to insert the needle always on the same side of the previous stitch.

24. **The WIDE GOBELIN STITCH is a straight stitch taken in a proportion that establishes an oblique angle less than 45 degrees.** Thus, it can be worked over two weft and one warp, **D**, or over three weft and two warp, **E**. There are many choices of method for working. This stitch can be worked in horizontal rows, **F**. Travel from left to right working the oblique stitch from bottom to top, **1A-1B** and from right to left working from top to bottom, **2A-2B**. Work the stitch on the diagonal, **G**. After completion of stitch **1A-1B,** pass under two warp threads before working stitch **2A-2B**. On the down journey, work each stitch from top to bottom, **3A-3B,** and pass two warp threads to the right before working stitch **4A-4B**. By holding the mesh correctly in an upright position, this stitch produces horizontal ridges. To produce vertical ridges, do not turn the mesh, but reverse the direction, not the working of the stitch, itself, **H**. The first stitch **1A-1B** is taken from the upper left to the lower right and the next stitch, **2A-2B** is worked after passing up, behind two weft threads. On the down journey, take the stitches from the lower right to the upper left, **3A-3B**.

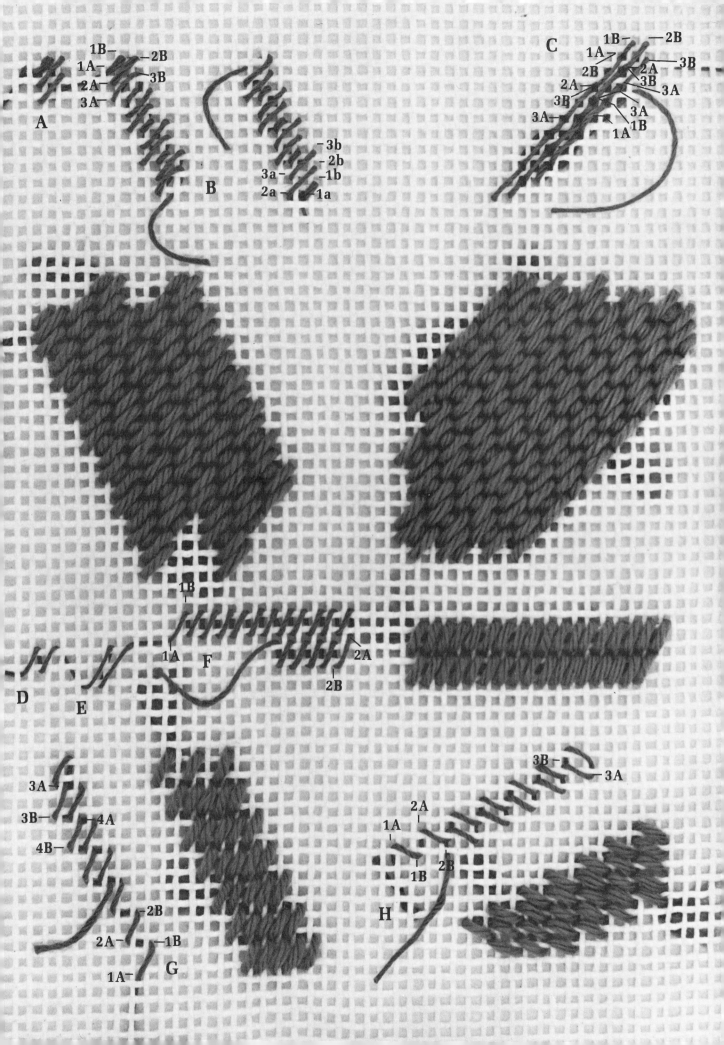

A

1B — — 2B
1A — — 3B
2A —
3A —

B

3a — — 3b
     — 2b
2a — — 1b
     — 1a

C

1B — — 2B
1A — — 3B
2B — — 2A
2A — — 3B
3B — — 3A
3A —   3A
        1A 1B

D

E

F

1B

1A

2A

2B

3A —   — 3B
3B —   — 4A   — 3A
4B —

2A
1A — — 1B
— 1B   2B

H

— 2B
2A — — 1B
1A — G

25. **The ENCROACHING GOBELIN STITCHES, A, are usually worked at a slight slant, over one warp thread.** Encroaching is useful for a soft blending of colors. Any of the Gobelin Stitches may be encroached, but the one shown is the most common. Take the stitch over any odd number of weft or horizontal mesh threads. Encroach the stitches of each new row over one weft thread on a consistent side of the stitch from the preceding row. Bring the needle up in an empty space and put it down next to the existent thread.

26. **ENCROACHING DOUBLE FLAT STITCH, B, is worked on the same principle as the Encroaching Gobelin.** The entire repeat of a Double Flat Stitch, whose three stitches usually utilize two vertical rows of spaces, now are encroached and occupy only one vertical row. The two separated short stitches are worked over an odd number of weft threads. The single long stitch is worked over either an even or odd number of weft threads depending on the count of threads separating the twin stitches. Each encroaches on the next by a count of half of one less than the total stitch count. For example, if the short stitches pass over three weft threads, the stitches encroach by one. If the short stitches pass over five weft threads, the stitches encroach by two. Adjacent rows also encroach, making the Encroaching Double Flat Stitch a good choice for blending colors. Caution is required to encroach consistently on the same side of neighboring stitches, while working in the rhythm of a Double Flat Stitch (a Darning Stitch) going always forward. Pull up **2A-2B** after bringing the needle up for **3A**, thus ensuring that the thread will not be split.

27. **PLAITED GOBELIN STITCHES are the result of both separating stitches and alternating the direction of rows of oblique stitches.** Plaited Gobelin Stitches are another excellent choice for blending colors. The stitches must be separated from each other by at least two warp threads to leave a space for the stitch of the subsequent row and the stitch, itself, must pass over an even count of weft threads to leave a central space. In the illustration, **C**, each individual stitch is taken over four weft threads and two warp threads, slanted either to the left or the right. From the top of the area, work the first row of stitches in the order shown by **1A-1B, 2A-2B.** The position of the stitches in the following row is illustrated by **1a-1b, 2a-2b.** Note that in each stitch the "**A**" is in an unused space and the "**B**" in a used space. **1a** of the second row is two spaces below **1A** of the first row. The "**B**" of a stitch goes into a space used by an "**A**" of a stitch two rows previous—one that slants in the same direction.

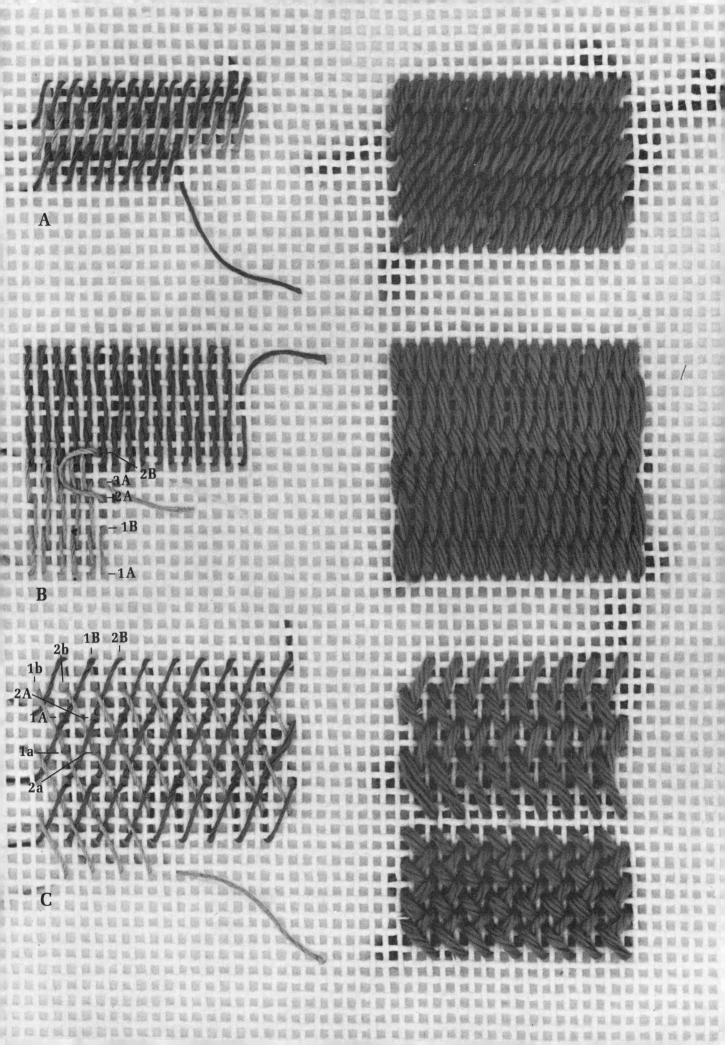

A

B

3A
2B
2A

1B

1A

2b
1B 2B
1b
2A
1A
1a

2a

C

28. The DIAGONAL PATTERN, A, is composed of diagonal rows of diagonal stitches whose order begins with a Tent Stitch, 1A-1B, and evenly expands, 2A-2B, 3A-3B, until it crosses four intersections of warp and weft threads, 4A-4B. The stitches then decrease in length until reaching the Tent Stitch. Each square on the diagonal shares a Tent Stitch with its neighbor. Starting at the lower right of a square, the mental picture is of the "A's" moving along the horizontal and the "B's" along the vertical until the longest stitch has been worked. Then, direction reverses and the "A's" move along the vertical and the "B's" along the horizontal. This method is a good choice for diagonal stripes between lower right and upper left.

The rows from upper left to lower right lie at a 45 degree angle. The rows from left to right are composed of squares that mount up one weft thread a unit. Consequently this pattern may also be worked with diagonal rows of Back Stitches of varying length, **B**, making this a suitable choice for diagonal stripes between the lower left and upper right.

29. The MOORISH PATTERN is a simple combination of rows of the Diagonal Pattern alternated with the Tent Stitch. Work these diagonal rows from the upper left to the lower right or from the lower right to the upper left, C.

Any number of rows of Tent Stitches may alternate with rows of Diagonal Pattern to fill an area.

The Moorish Pattern may also be worked with diagonal rows of Back Stitches traveling from the upper right to the lower left, or the reverse.

30. The SCOTTISH PATTERN is oriented to the vertical and horizontal lines of the mesh, D. The stitches are once more a combination of the Diagonal Pattern and the Tent Stitch. Each square of the Diagonal Pattern is separated; consequently, each square contains its own Tent Stitch at the beginning and ending. The squares are positioned as on a checkerboard. They are separated on all sides from their neighboring squares by one row of Tent Stitch. Complete the Scottish Pattern by first working all the squares of Diagonal Pattern, then fill in the horizontal and, lastly, the vertical Continental Tent Stitches.

The Scottish may also be worked with diagonal rows of Back Stitches from the upper right to the lower left, or the reverse.

31. The CHECKER PATTERN enlarges on the area covered by the Tent Stitch in the Scottish Pattern. One isolated square of Diagonal Pattern alternates with one isolated square of Tent Stitches, **E**. The horizontal rows, squared units of diagonal stitches, are worked most easily from right to left and then left to right. The stitch order is important. It is essential to know how to work the Basketweave Tent Stitch beginning in any corner. The illustration is of, first, the order from the left to the right and, second, from right to left. The arrow shows where the sequence begins. Each stitch customarily begins in the lower left, slanting towards and ending in the upper right.

The Checker Pattern may be worked with diagonal rows of Back Stitches traveling from the upper right to the lower left or the reverse.

A

4B
3B
2B
1B

4A 3A 2A 1A

B

C

D

E

32. **The VANDYKE PATTERN is one of the many counted patterns which can be devised or varied.** It is composed of a triangular unit of straight, whipped stitches that form an effective, but loose surface. Its appearance is much altered by color distribution and stitch proportion. The standard triangle of the VanDyke Pattern is composed of stitches over one, five, nine, and thirteen weft threads. It can be diminished by a count of over one, three, five, and seven weft threads, **A**. The color can be solid to form a quilt-like surface. Zigzag vertical ribbons appear if the triangles are worked in horizontal rows of alternate colors, reversed in the following row, **B**. Straight-edged vertical stripes appear by working every horizontal row in the same order of alternating colors, **C**.

Vertical stripes are also formed with vertical rows of Back Stitches worked in the following count before any color is changed: first row, over one and seven; second row, over three and five; third row, over five and three; fourth row, over seven and one. An interesting effect quite different from the others results from working each triangle of a horizontal row in one color, **D**. After studying this, devise other secondary patterns by changing the color of individual triangular units.

The entire pattern can be composed of horizontal stitches.

33. **The MILANESE PATTERN is the VanDyke Pattern worked on the diagonal.** Working complete diagonal rows in alternate colors produces jagged diagonal lines up to the left, **E**. Working the complete diagonal rows in equal alternating colored units produces smooth lines up to the right, **F**. These may easily be worked using the Back Stitch on the diagonal from upper right to lower left. Working each complete diagonal row in the opposite alternate colors as its neighboring rows produces interesting effects and patterns, **G**.

A   B   C   D

E   F   G

34. **The HONEYCOMB PATTERN is a detached patterning formed by initially laying an evenly spaced grid of horizontal and, over them, vertical lines.** Tie these together into a honeycombed surface with diagonal lines that begin and end at the sides of the horizontals and verticals. Weave these through the existing threads, passing over each vertical and under each horizontal, **A**.

Laying a base of horizontal, vertical, or diagonal lines and working stitches over them creates interesting effects unrelated to the size of the underlying mesh. The following are all weaving techniques, usually used for flat-woven rugs. The laid threads represent the warp on the loom.

35. **The DETACHED STEM STITCH is shown, B; it may be worked this way in a small area.** Bring the needle out beneath the lowest laid thread at the left side. Loop the needle up over this first base thread and down beneath with the point emerging to the right of the looping thread. Continue to the top of the area, working the Stem Stitch over each successive laid thread. Begin the next line once more below the base row or loop it in reversed direction from the top.

36. **The PADDED WIDE STEM STITCH, worked over the laid threads and through the mesh, is used in any but a small area, C.** Note that **1A** emerges below the lowest laid thread in one vertical row of spaces and **1B** goes to the back above the second laid thread and in the neighboring vertical row of spaces. **2A** emerges in the initial vertical row in the space beneath the second laid thread. The needle is brought out on the side which is the direction traveled from and the rhythm continues to the end of one row of Padded Wide Stem Stitches. Each row may be worked in a different color. Each row may be reversed, **D**, in which case some spacing adjustment becomes necessary.

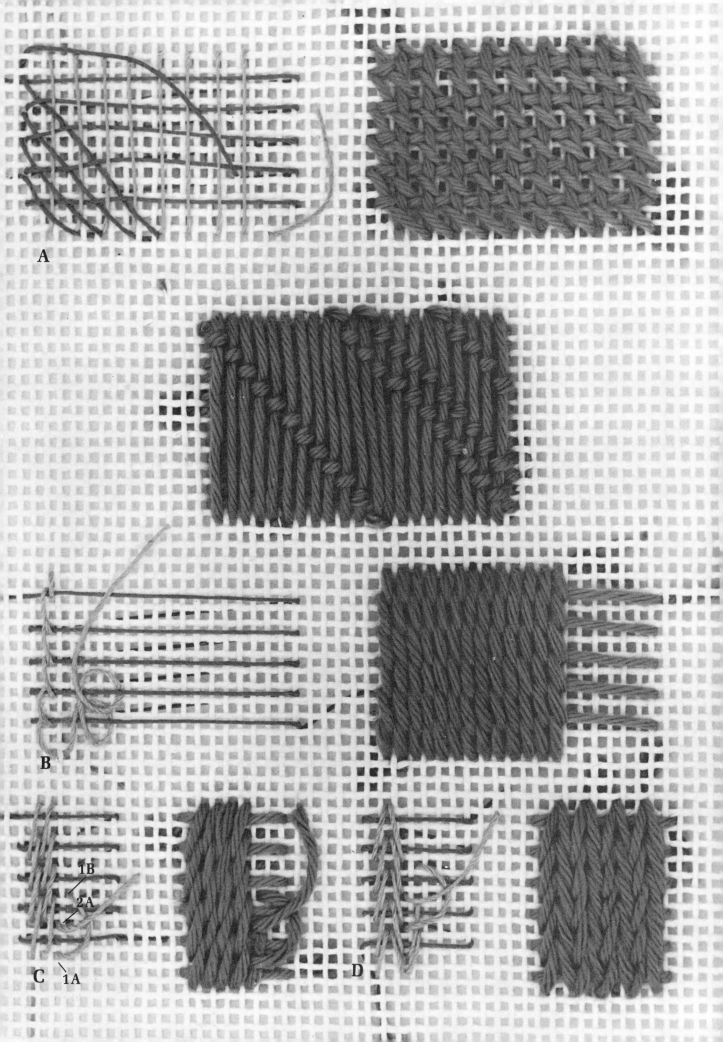

A

B

C 1B 2A 1A

D

The **OPEN BURDEN PATTERN** on mesh differs slightly from that on a closed fabric but the appearance is the same. The Burden is an imitation of a basketwoven or "plainweave" surface. In Meshwork, while the surface must be completely covered, the proportion and relative positions of verticals and horizontals may still change.

37. **The surface may be covered with an OPEN, DETACHED BURDEN PATTERN which is actually darned, A.** Lay the horizontals, **1A-1B, 2A-2B**, spaced as desired to fit the area or the size of the yarn. Cross these with vertical, darned rows. These may be spaced differently from the horizontal rows and be worked of differently colored or sized yarns.

When the Burden Pattern is detached from the surface of the mesh, the entire area should be small. If large, the method must change into a padded technique.

A balanced basketwoven surface is best achieved by working the Basketweave Tent Stitch on the reverse side of the fabric.

38. **Any proportion other than even is better worked as an OPEN, PADDED BURDEN PATTERN, B.** The horizontals are laid on the surface and couched down by individual vertical stitches which come up and go back down under the laid horizontals. Since the one space is used, these individual vertical stitches must be worked horizontally, **1A-1B, 2A-2B**. All the horizontals may be laid and then the verticals stitched or one horizontal may be couched at a time. Think of the Burden Pattern as a padded, open Gobelin Pattern. Try patterning with these stitches. Inspiration for them may be found in books of weaving drafts or of actual basketweaving.

39. **The DIAGONAL BURDEN PATTERN may also be worked detached or padded, utilizing the same two procedures on the diagonal, C and D.** In order to avoid confusion, the second, padded method may have each diagonal row couched individually. In **C**, note that straight diagonal darning rows that begin in adjacent diagonal spaces end in every other space along vertical or horizontal rows. **D** is illustrated with the laid diagonal beginning and ending in every other space on the horizontal and vertical edges. Each stitch crossing the laid thread emerges from beneath the thread above and passes to the back behind the one below. In order to create the woven appearance, place the couching stitches in every other diagonal space. The first method produces a flatter surface than the second.

1A
2A
1B
2B

A

2B
1B
1A
2A

B

D

C

40. **The CLOSED STRIPED BURDEN PATTERNS are all composed of Double Running Stitches.** In addition, in the Closed, Detached Burden Patterns the working threads are twisted. This is a new technique. A horizontally striped, Closed, Detached Burden Pattern, **A**, utilizes two differently colored yarns threaded into two needles, #1 and #2, in the same vertical row over the laid threads. The weaving yarn should be thick and the laid threads thin to enable the first to move in over the second. In small areas, only, bring both needles to the surface through the identical space at the upper left, above the first laid thread. Weave needle 1 under and over the first two laid threads. Weave needle #2 over and under the same two laid threads and then pass needle #2 to the left under needle #1. This places it to the right of needle #2 ready to pass over the second laid thread. Continue to the end of the row, alternating needle #1 and #2. Begin each row over again at the top and repeat the order for horizontal stripes. The patterning needle, the one that passes over the laid thread, is always on the right and always passes over and then under the laid thread and then under the other needle. The twisting holds the alternating threads securely in position.

For a diagonally striped, Closed, Detached Burden Pattern, **B**, alternate the order of the needles in each row.

For a vertically striped, Closed, Detached Burden Pattern, use the same color for both journeys in alternate rows, **C**. This may be facilitated by using four needles, two of each color. See illustration.

In a large area, striped, Closed, Padded Burden Pattern anchors the stitches to the mesh.

Double Running Stitches of one color are used which, traveling from top to bottom and bottom to top, emerge from below and beneath a laid thread, cross the next laid thread and go to the back above and beneath the third laid thread. When a row (two journeys) of one color is completed, every other laid thread remains exposed. The stitches of the second color travel in the same row from bottom to top and top to bottom, utilizing the alternate laid threads. Upon the completion of the two complete rows, all laid threads are covered. Since the effect is gained from padding and the stitches are attached, the laid threads may be thick. To maintain a straight vertical line and duplicate the appearance of the Detached Closed Burden, each stitch of the second color emerges on one constant side of the preceding stitch and goes to the back on the opposite side of the next. For a horizontally striped, Closed, Padded Burden Pattern, **D**, begin each row with the same color.

For a diagonally striped, Closed, Padded Burden Pattern, **E**, reverse the order of colors in each row.

For a vertically striped, Closed, Padded Burden Pattern, **F**, work each complete row of Double Running Stitches in a single color, alternating colors in adjacent rows.

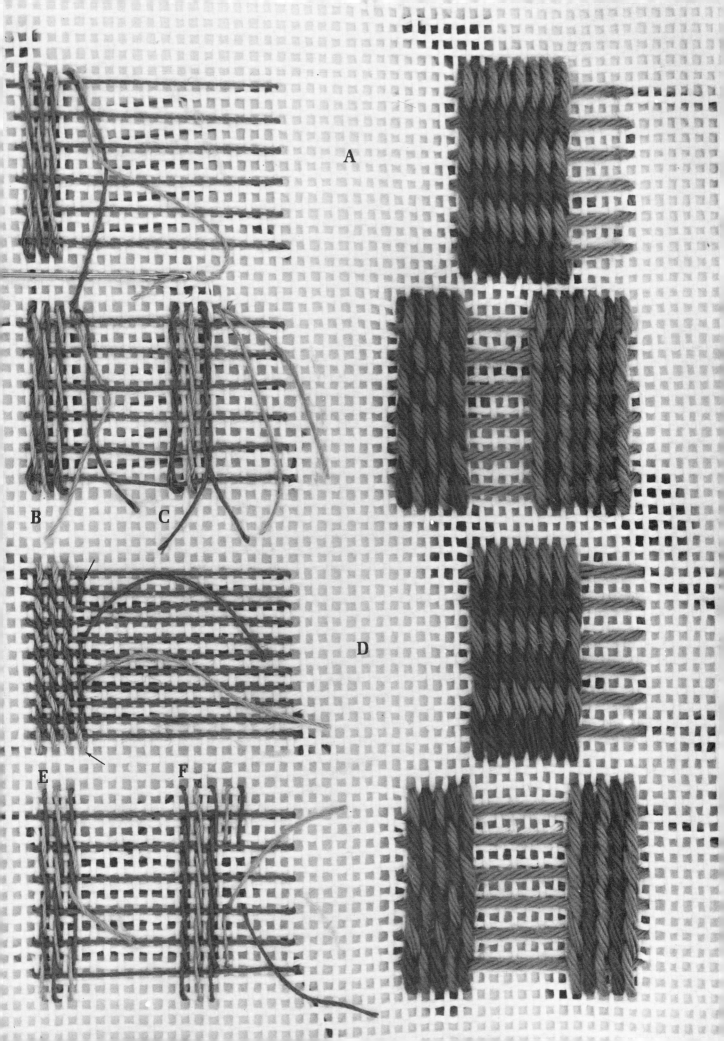

41. **When the Burden Pattern is enlarged in the horizontal direction, only, it produces another woven effect which is MULTIPLE AND UNBALANCED.** In illustration **A**, there are three vertical stitches over four weft threads to one horizontal. The base threads are initially laid every other row so that each will pass alternately under the center of one row of vertical units and between two vertical units. The base thread is couched down by the units of three vertical stitches. These are easily worked on the diagonal from upper left to lower right. The vertical and the horizontal proportion may be reversed.

42. **Illustration B is the same pattern without the base threads. This is often called the Algerian Pattern, but is actually a MULTIPLE GOBELIN.** For added design, work units in varying colors.

43. **The horizontal stitches in a unit may be multiplied to the same number as the verticals to produce a MULTIPLE, BALANCED BURDEN PATTERN.** In illustration **C**, the base threads are laid across every row and the vertical units are separated to create an evenly balanced surface.

44. **If the area is large, both the vertical and the horizontal units are composed of individual stitches, creating an equally even surface, the CLOSED BASKET PATTERN, D.** The units encroach by one thread. Each stitch crosses over as many spaces as there are stitches in the opposing unit. Note that in the actual working order, stitches go to the back under preceding ones and emerge in empty spaces.

The vertical stitches define the horizontal strips and the horizontal stitches define the vertical strips. The "basket" effect is drawn with the whipped stitches rather than truly woven.

45. **The OPEN BASKET PATTERN, E, is balanced.** The resultant squares may be filled with any choice of stitches, such as Tent Stitches, Diagonal Pattern, or Crosses in Squares. The proportion changes to accommodate other patterns in the openings. The proportion also changes when more complex basketweave patterns, knotwork and fretwork patterns are established.

46. **A CLOSED MULTIPLE BASKET PATTERN occurs when each horizontal and vertical strip is multiplied, F.** Stitches in the opposing direction begin and end with the first and last spaces covered by individual stitches in a unit. Careful graphing and placement imparts the woven appearance.

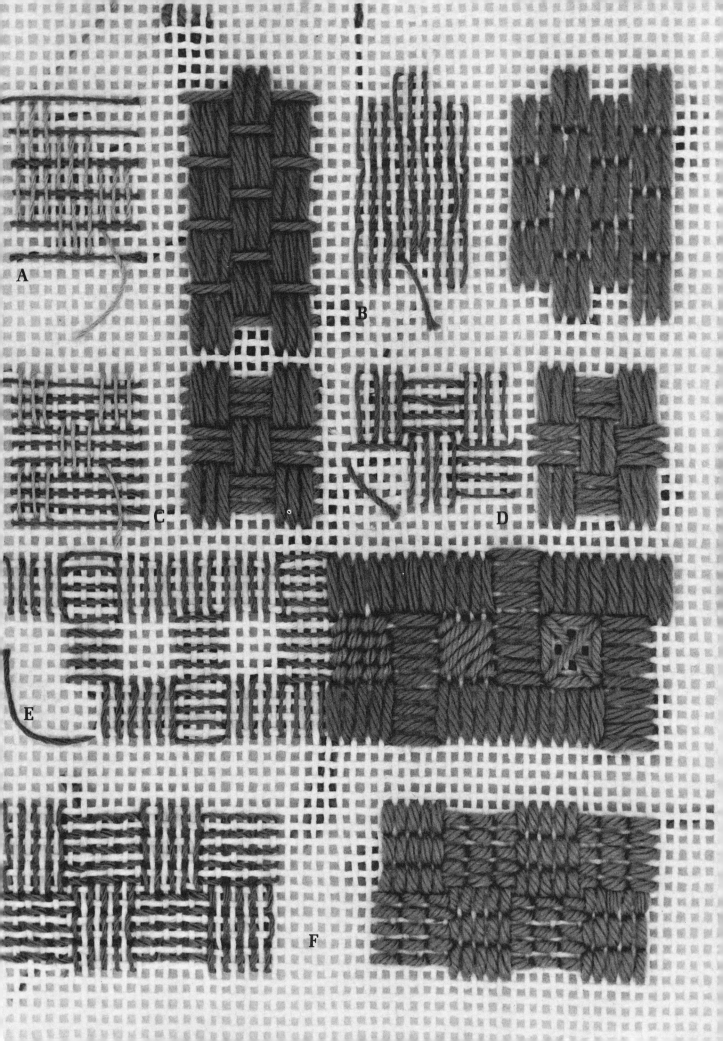

47. The PERSPECTIVE PATTERN must begin with the lower diagonal stitches and build towards the top. The centers may be filled with Tent Stitch. The length of a stitch and the number of stitches are the same; if a stitch crosses four intersections, there are four stitches in a unit, **A.**

48. The OPEN PERSPECTIVE or FANCY PATTERN is the Perspective Pattern turned on its side and worked with no overlapping, **B.** A ric-rac ribbon effect is produced by each zig-zag stripe of one color, **C.** A three dimensional illusion is achieved when all diagonals on the same slant are worked in the same color, **D.** The center spaces may be filled in any manner consistent with the effect and two possibilities are shown here.

49. The DOUBLE STAR PATTERN has been developed from the Open Perspective Pattern. Because the repeat of this pattern is large, the two variations are illustrated only by diagram. This pattern is lovely worked in covering threads of different colors. In **E** is shown the Open Perspective Pattern worked twice in perpendicular relationship. In **F**, one vertical row of stars is dropped down one-half and also moved in towards an existing vertical row of stars. The original row is worked in a different color thread than the two adjoining it on either side, in half-drop position.

50. **The PALACE PATTERN is an interesting, damask-like pattern that can be greatly changed through placement of color, A.** The surface pattern consists of two sizes of units taken from the center of the Open Perspective Pattern, positioned alternately horizontally and vertically. The remaining areas can be filled with straight diagonal stitches or Tent Stitches. The yarn may need plying up for complete coverage. Note that the horizontal stitches appear more separated than the vertical even when seen from a 90 degree turned viewing position.

51. **The VANDYKE SQUARE PATTERN is a series of units, like those used in the Open Perspective Pattern and the Palace Pattern, joined to each other at right angles, B.** Within each unit there are two VanDyke shapes back to back. Omitting the shortest stitch in each VanDyke leaves squared shapes to be filled with other stitches, **C.** The unit may also be halved into individual VanDyke shapes worked with straight stitches directed towards the point. Four of these meeting at a common center form a square. The design unit may then be this square, **D.** Omitting the shortest stitch in each VanDyke shape also leaves squared shapes to be filled, **E.** One unit of these two VanDykes may be considered the design unit.

52. **The DARMSTADT PATTERN is yet another way to alter the unit formed by the VanDyke Square.** This is accomplished by breaking up the longer stitches at the center as illustrated in **F.** These units in repeat share the shortest end stitch with their neighbors. Bricked rows are repeated, **G**, or alternate rows are worked in which the stitch direction is reversed, **H.** These new units are actually one stitch shorter than the others. In the illustration, note that the longest stitch is taken over less threads than is the previous unit. The total, however, is a square.

53. **The SHEAF PATTERN is worked with units of long, encroaching Upright Gobelin Stitches.** It is illustrative of the decisions often necessary to adjust a pleasing pattern to cover mesh. If the tie-down stitch about the center of a sheaf is precisely centered, there must be a central space behind the sheaf. The uneven number of Upright Gobelin Stitches must extend over an even number of weft threads to cover an uneven number of spaces. **A** illustrates this plan. The adjoining row must be worked in half-drop position. The "join" of two sheaves in a vertical row is a line beneath the encroaching stitches. The central stitch tying a sheaf is over a space. Since a space cannot be centered on a line, some adjustment becomes necessary. In **B**, each Upright Gobelin extends over seven weft threads. The central space is judged to be in the vertical row beneath the center stitch and up a count of three spaces. While this is somewhat arbitrary, the decision does center the next vertical row of sheaves correctly next to the first. We choose to use this count for the most even coverage.

Begin at the base of a row and whip five stitches into place. Above these, work five more stitches, encroaching on one side of the stitches in the first group by one thread. Continue until the top of the area is reached.

Bring the needle through from the back at the center of a unit. Place the point of the needle behind the stitches on top of the mesh. Tie the stitches together by passing the needle behind the stitches on the left, across the top of all of them and behind the stitches on the right. Put the needle through to the back at the center of the unit and gently pull up the sheaf. Pass to the unit above and continue to make sheaves of each unit of stitches.

The next vertical row is formed of sheaves in a half-drop position and begins after passing three weft threads from the start of the first row.

When the area has been filled, the tie-down stitches might also be threaded as shown. This emphasizes the existing pattern.

54. **The SHELL PATTERN is a variation of the Sheaf Pattern.** It is worked in horizontal rows of level sheaves, **C**. The count of each stitch is taken over an even number of weft threads, a count of six being used in the illustration. The yarn might be of more plys than that used for the Sheaf Pattern. Each sheaf is tied before progressing to the following unit.

The sheaves are then double threaded with one color of the same ply yarn or threaded in two journeys, using two colors, **D**.

55. **The LEAF PATTERN is formed of Straight Stitches taken from the outer border to the center.** The logical working order of the stitches is shown by the singly numbered leaf. The leaves in this illustration, **E**, are in connected diagonal rows worked from the upper left to the lower right.

A   B

C   D

E

2 1 7
3   8
4   9
5 —   — 10
6 —
  1 11

56. **The CROSS STITCH is the old favorite, Gros Point, that your ancestors used as the standard stitch on mesh rather than the Tent Stitch.** The Tent Stitch is the top, second stitch of the Cross Stitch. When the Cross Stitch is used, a balanced symmetrical coverage of mesh is the result so any design can be accurately reproduced. The Cross Stitch is the most important Meshwork stitch. It is simple to paint color designations directly onto the mesh by placing a spot of color on the central intersections of warp and weft threads beneath each cross. The same is true of the graph paper in a cartoon.

In all Cross Stitches, the top stitch's slant is the same, traditionally from lower left to upper right. The Cross Stitch is worked in either of two methods. One, by completing one cross before beginning the next, working from right to left or left to right in horizontal rows, from bottom to top or top to bottom in vertical rows. Two, by working the first half of the cross along a row and then traveling back working the final half of the cross. The first method is the recommended one.

To work one Cross Stitch at a time from right to left, **A**, begin in the lower right corner, **1A**, and cross to **1B**. Return to the *starting side*, **2A**, and complete the top stitch, **2B**. Bring the needle up once more in **2A**, ready for the next Cross Stitch on the left.

To work one Cross Stitch at a time from left to right, reverse the procedure, **B**. Adjacent rows are worked back and forth by combining these two.

To work one Cross Stitch at a time from the bottom to the top, **C**, begin at the lower right corner, **1A**, and cross to **1B**. Bring the needle out opposite at **2A** and cross to **2B**. Return to **2A**, ready for the next complete cross.

To work one complete Cross Stitch at a time from top to bottom, reverse the procedure, **D**. Use the two orders together to work continuous down and up journeys.

To work a row from right to left and back, two journeys, **E**, begin at the lower right corner, **1A**, and cross to **1B**. Return to the starting side, **2A**, and cross to **2B**. Continue to the end of the row. The return journey begins, **1a**, at the lower left corner and crosses the former stitch to **1b**, emerging below at the starting side, **2a**, ready to complete the next cross.

To work a row from left to right and back, two journeys, reverse the procedure, **F**.

When working an area from the top down, use method **E**; when working from the lower area up, use method **F**.

To work a row from bottom to top and back, two journeys, **G**, begin at the lower right, **1A**, and cross to **1B**. Emerge opposite at **2A**, ready for the next diagonal. The return journey begins at **1a**, crosses the former stitch, **1b**, emerging opposite at **2a** for the next diagonal stitch.

To work a row from top to bottom and back, two journeys, reverse the working procedure, **H**.

When working an area from left towards right, use method **G**; when working from the right towards the left, use method **H**.

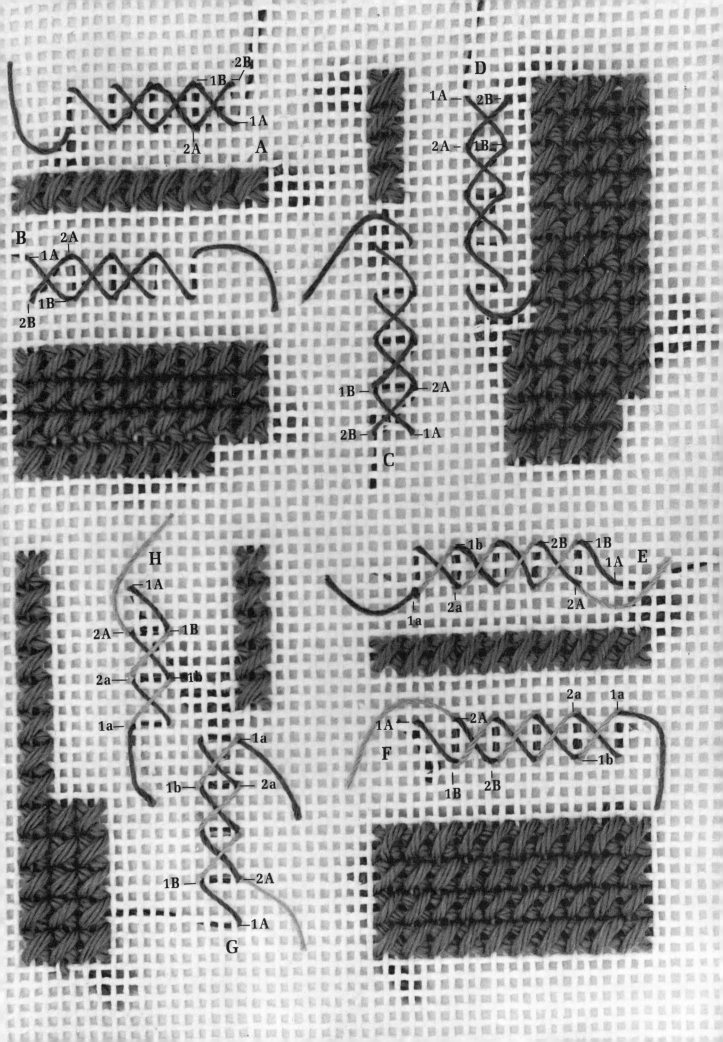

57. The **DIAGONAL CROSS STITCH is worked by two methods in diagonal rows.** The first is by completing each cross in a single journey and the other is by completing the cross in two journeys.

For the first, work a diagonal row from the lower right, **A**, beginning at the lower right corner of the cross, **1A**, and crossing to **1B**. Bring the needle out at the *starting side*, **2A**, and cross to **2B**. Emerge at **1B**, ready for the next Cross Stitch. After completion of the first row, begin the next down row with a Cross Stitch placed immediately above or below the final one of the previous row, **B**. The first half of the stitch is worked in the reverse direction but the second half still travels from the lower left to the upper right, **1a-1b-2a-2b**, emerging at **1b** for the next switch.

The second method is, like the Diagonal Tent Stitch, worked with a series of Back Stitches in diagonal rows, **C**. Begin at the lower side of the area with the upper left of the first stitch, **1A**, cross to **1B** and emerge in the upper left of the next stitch, **2A**. Fill the entire area with these diagonal rows of Back Stitches. Then, begin at the upper side of the area and cross these with rows of Back Stitches on the opposing diagonal lines, **1a-1b-2a-2b**.

58. The **UPRIGHT CROSS STITCH crosses on the vertical and the horizontal.** It might be considered as a regular Cross Stitch placed on the diagonal. It can be worked in vertical, horizontal, or diagonal rows.

In **D**, the horizontal method is illustrated. Work the vertical stitch, **1A-1B**, and then bring the needle up on the side of the vertical stitch from which you are traveling, **2A**. In the illustration, this is from the right. Be careful to always bring the needle up on a constant side of the preceding stitch that has used the same space. After crossing the first stitch to **2B**, bring the needle up for **3A** after passing diagonally behind the count of intersections equal to one-half the length of a stitch.

In **E**, the diagonal and preferred method is illustrated. Starting in any corner, bring the needle up at the starting point, **1A**, and down, **1B**, the length of a vertical stitch. Unlike the regular Cross Stitch, the Upright Cross Stitch must be worked over an even count of threads to leave a central row. Bring the needle up for **2A** on the side of the vertical stitch in the direction the row is traveling. In the illustration, this is towards the upper left. Cross over the first stitch, **2B**, and bring the needle back up in **2A**, ready for the next Upright Cross Stitch. In subsequent rows, arrange the order so that **1B** and **2B** go down to the back in spaces already filled, rather than to the front.

F illustrates the vertical method. Bring the needle up, **1A**, at the starting point and down, **1B**, in the direction the row is traveling. Bring the needle up, **2A**, on either side, preferably in an empty space, cross over the first stitch, **2B**, and come back out at **1B**, ready for the next Cross Stitch.

B

1a
2b
2a
1b
1B
2B
1A
2A A

1b
1a
2b
2a
2A
1A
1B
C

2B
1B
2A
3A
1A
D

1B
2B
2A
1A
E

1B
2A 2A
2B 2B
1A
F

59. The OBLONG CROSS STITCH is an elongated Cross Stitch. It is worked in an oblong rather than a square. It may be worked like any of the other Cross Stitches as well as in interesting new combinations. Through these, the Oblong Cross Stitch leads into and becomes other distinct stitches. The Oblong Cross Stitch is, therefore, an important one.

Begin as shown in **A** with the Oblong Cross Stitch worked in horizontal rows both from right to left, **1A-1B-2A-2B-3A**, and from left to right, **1a-1b-2a-2b-3a**.

Work the stitches on what is an approximation of a diagonal, **B**, up as in **1A-1B-2A-2B-3A** and down as in **1a-1b-2a-2b-3a**.

Illustration **C** demonstrates the stitch order for covering the ground with rows of Oblong Crosses arranged in half-drop position. The cross must lie over an even number of weft threads. Another effective pattern is created by working a second layer of Oblong Crosses over the first, the second layer being positioned in half-drop position to the first layer, **D**.

The crosses can lie in a horizontal oblong as well as a vertical one.

Try placing the Oblong Crosses diagonally on the mesh. Diagonal rows are worked in the same manner as the former horizontal rows, **E**. Vertical rows are worked in the same manner as the former diagonal rows, **F**.

Once the area has been filled, using any working order, either or both the centers of the crosses and the horizontal join line between crosses may be covered with Back Stitches.

The Oblong Cross may overlap vertically, **G**, forming another attractive filling. If the stitch has been worked over an even number of warp threads, it may also overlap horizontally, **H**. It is at this point, when the horizontally overlapping Oblong Cross Stitch is worked in continuous rows, either horizontal, vertical, or diagonal, that it actually becomes another stitch named the Basket Stitch.

The regular Cross Stitch joins well with the vertical and the horizontal Oblong Cross Stitch and the regular Cross Stitch and the Upright Cross Stitch join well with the diagonal Oblong Cross Stitch.

60. The RICE STITCH is also, most appropriately, named the Crossed Corners Cross Stitch. It is an excellent choice of a sturdy stitch with an interesting texture for a rug. The "ricing" may be worked over the arms of any Cross Stitch large enough to have remaining a central space between the ends of the arms. While many older sources recommend using a heavy thread for the large Cross Stitch and a fine one for the crossed corners, it seems better if both journeys are worked with the same thickness, less than the ply normally used for a corresponding Cross Stitch, alone.

When the regular Cross Stitches or Oblong Cross Stitches openly cover the entire ground, the crossed corners may be worked with lines of Back Stitches worked on the diagonal, as the Diagonal Tent Stitch, **I**.

When the crossed corners on one cross are finished before proceeding to the next, a series of Back Stitches are also utilized, this time encircling the cross. While any order may be used, one choice for working an area diagonally up from the lower right to the upper left is illustrated in **J**, as well as the reverse movement traveling back down from upper left to lower right, **K**.

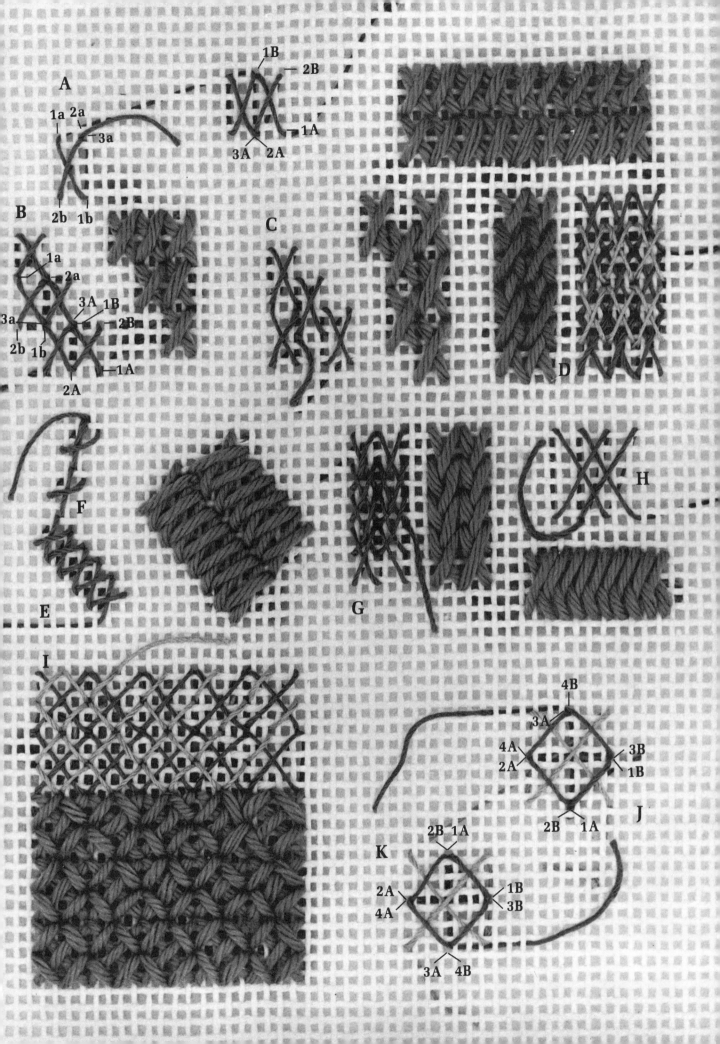

Sampler Pattern